DRAGONS AND SILK

FROM THE FORBIDDEN CITY

 THE GENIUS OF CHINA   A CLOSE-UP GUIDE

DRAGONS AND SILK FROM THE FORBIDDEN CITY

 The art of Chinese embroidery predates painting in early China and has always been considered one of the highest art forms. Beauty and magic were associated with silk in early times. 'We . . . . dressed ourselves like flowers in embroidered clothing,' recorded a shaman describing a ritual during the Han Dynasty (206BC-AD220).

The production of silk extends back to 2000BC, when Xiling Shi, the consort of the legendary Yellow Emperor, was said to have discovered how to make silk cloth from the silkworm cocoon. One of the earliest surviving pieces of evidence of silk weaving is a Shang Dynasty (*c.* 1600-1027BC) fragment, transmuted in the patina of two bronzes.

In ancient times silk was as precious as gold. The secret of its manufacture was not discovered in the West until the Middle Ages. Indeed it was for the purpose of acquiring China's fabulous silks that the trade routes between East and West were first opened.

Over 2,000 years of painstaking labour has left us with a collection of work that reflects the cosmic philosophies, the poetry and the power of China. Some of the finest embroideries were made for the Imperial Court in the Forbidden City, where the palace studio employed thousands of artisans to produce robes and hangings for the imperial family's personal use.

*Yellow embroidered **jifu** with the 12 symbols of authority, c. 1820,*
made for Emperor Daoguang (reigned 1821–1851).

JIFU : FORMAL COURT DRAGON ROBE

The emperor, princes and mandarins wore these fine silk robes as emblems of their office. (Mandarins were civil and military officials, appointed through a strict and rigorous public examination process. Their advancement depended on merit.) The strict ceremonial laws of the Qing Dynasty (1644-1911), established in 1759 and enforced in 1766, required that mandarins wore robes covered in dragons and other symbols for all formal and ceremonial occasions. These robes are known as *longpao* or dragon robes.

The ancient Chinese believed that dragons were benevolent creatures whose breath turned into clouds and whose power manifested itself in thunder and rain. The dragon also represented storms, good luck, virility, authority and the creative, dynamic force in the universe. From the Han Dynasty (206BC-AD220) onwards, dragons were the symbol of the emperor and the Qing imperial dragon was distinguished by having five claws. There are always nine dragons on the *jifu*, with the ninth hidden in the fold; nine is an auspicious number denoting virility and power. The dragons are shown either holding or chasing the Flaming Pearl of

Detail of jifu *in red-brown embroidered silk, the nine dragons couched in gold. This robe is also decorated with cranes (longevity) and the* ji *character (luck), which together mean hope for a long life.* c. 1880.

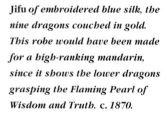

Jifu of embroidered blue silk, the nine dragons couched in gold. This robe would have been made for a high-ranking mandarin, since it shows the lower dragons grasping the Flaming Pearl of Wisdom and Truth. c. 1870.

An embroidered brown satin silk jifu *with nine gold couched dragons and ribbed indigo silk sleeves embroidered with bats. There were five shades of yellow; brown, being a 'lesser yellow', was worn by members of the imperial clan. c. 1770.*

Wisdom and Truth. This symbolizes the wearer's desire to attain inner wisdom.

The design represents a diagram of the universe, the combination of symbols having cosmic significance. At the hem of the robe is the *lishui* border, represented by diagonal stripes for water, and above that is the sea with its rolling waves. The Earth-Mountains are represented by four tall mountain peaks. The air element and clouds are above the mountains and the neck of the robe represents the Gate of Heaven. The symbolism is completed when the robe is worn, with the wearer's head representing Heaven.

The court robes were designed, through the use of symbols, to reinforce the divine right of the emperor, who was regarded as a 'God on Earth'. Confucius (551-479BC) once said of the emperor: 'Let his faculties and his virtues that are so powerful make him equal with Heaven.'

A mandarin wearing the dragon robe represented the authority of the emperor and carried the power to institute the will of the emperor and administer his laws and punishments.

Winter jifu *of deep blue satin silk with nine gold couched dragons surrounded by auspicious emblems. Trimmed with fur. c. 1850.*

Imperial Robes with the 12 Symbols of Authority

Confucius, in his *Analects*, describes the relationship between dress and *li* (righteousness):

> 'He (the emperor) adjusts his clothes and cap and throws a dignity into his looks, so that thus dignified, he is looked at in awe — is not this to be majestic without being fierce?'

The style of the emperor's *jifu* and that of the princes and mandarins who served him was the same. In 1759 a law was passed whereby the emperor's robe had to be distinguished by the inclusion of the 12 signs of imperial authority. The incorporation of these symbols completed the message that the emperor had a mandate from Heaven to rule over all creation. These symbols had been used by the Ming (1368-1644) and previous dynasties, but had not been adopted by the Qing until decreed in 1759. The 12 symbols of authority were arranged in order of importance, in three rings falling at the neck, waist and knees.

The laws of the Qing Dynasty also required the emperor and empress to wear yellow robes for all special occasions. Exceptions were made for the four great annual sacrifices, when a specific colour was demanded by the occasion. These robes were very rare, being worn only for the specific ceremonies. Pale blue (or 'moon-white') robes were worn for sacrifices to the moon during the autumn equinox. *Lidong*, the start of winter, was the occasion for sacrifices to Heaven, when the emperor appealed for rain and a good harvest. At this time the emperor wore a dark blue robe symbolizing Heaven. Red robes were worn for the sacrifice to the sun at dawn on the spring equinox. Bright yellow robes were worn for sacrifices to the earth and to the imperial ancestors.

Detail from a yellow **kesi** *robe made for Emperor Guangxu (reigned 1875–1908).*

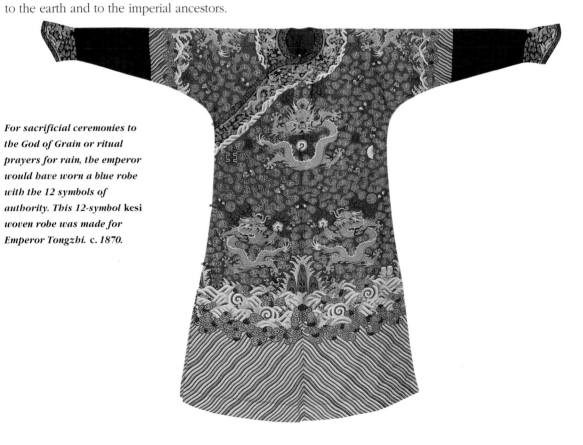

For sacrificial ceremonies to the God of Grain or ritual prayers for rain, the emperor would have worn a blue robe with the 12 symbols of authority. This 12-symbol **kesi** *woven robe was made for Emperor Tongzhi. c. 1870.*

The 12 Symbols of Authority

 The Sun – Located on the left shoulder, the sun is represented by a three-legged bird in a yellow disc, symbolizing Heaven and intellectual enlightenment. The number three is the symbol of the masculine principle, of which the sun is the essence.

 The Moon – On the right shoulder is a white moon disc, within which the Hare of the Moon is pounding with a pestle to obtain the elixir of immortality.

 Constellation – Above the principal dragon on the chest is an arrangement of three small discs, representing stars in a constellation and symbolic of Heaven and the cosmic universe.

 Mountains – Located on the back, above the principal dragon, are mountains, signifying the earth.

The sun, moon, constellation and mountains represented the four annual sacrifices made by the emperor and together indicated his authority over the whole universe.

 Pair of Dragons – These symbolize the emperor's adaptability through transformation or renewal.

 Pheasant – Exemplifies literary refinement and education.

 Fu – A character meaning discernment of good and evil or judgement.

 Axe – This denotes temporal power and justice in the punishment of crime.

 Water Weeds – The water weeds rise and fall with the seasons, representing responses to the needs of the moment.

 Libation Cups – A pair of bronze libation cups represent the element of metal and signify filial piety.

 Flames – Flames symbolize intellectual brilliance and zeal for virtue.

Grain – A plate of millet or grain denotes the emperor's responsibility to feed the people.

These 12 symbols completed the message that the emperor, the Son of Heaven, had control over all creation as regent for the Lord of Heaven.

Child's imperial robe of brown kesi *weave, with nine dragons, peonies and bats amongst clouds, 19th century.*

Yellow gauze summer robe worked with exquisitely fine double-sided embroidery; made for the Qianlong Empress, 18th century.

MAN'S *CHAO-FU* : CEREMONIAL COURT DRAGON ROBE

The *chaofu* was the most formal costume at the imperial court during the Qing Dynasty, being worn only 12 times a year at the principal sacrificial ceremonies conducted at dawn by the emperor himself. The torches held up high during the processions would have lit up the magnificent gold couched dragons, prominent against the deep indigo silk which merged with the darkness as the mandarins and princes accompanied the Son of Heaven to his annual sacrifices. Although it is the costume most frequently shown in Qing ancestor portraits, the *chaofu* is extremely rare, since only the most high-ranking mandarins were allowed to wear it.

The Ming Dynasty was ruled by emperors from the Han majority, an agricultural and sedentary people based around the fertile valleys of the Yangtze and Yellow Rivers of central China. The Ming Dynasty garments were made with voluminous amounts of silk, as this was a mark of refinement and elegance. The people who ended Ming rule and established the Qing Dynasty in 1644 were from Manchuria. These nomadic people from the cold steppes of north-central Asia were excellent and hardy equestrians. Their horses played a central role in their culture and they were able to ride long distances, hunting by bow and arrow. Their clothing, unlike that worn during the Ming Dynasty, reflected the need for freedom of movement, as well as the demands of keeping warm while spending long hours in the saddle. Close-fitting tunics, with long cuffs that covered the hands resting on the pommel of the saddle, were features of the Manchu national costume. These 'horseshoe'–shaped cuffs were cut to protect the backs of the hands, while still allowing the fingers to work the reins. Below the tunic, the Manchu warrior wore leggings covered by a pair of pleated 'aprons', open in the middle and back.

The cut of the *chaofu* was based on this traditional Manchu riding outfit, though modified somewhat for the more sedate demands of court and diplomacy. From the outset, the Manchus were determined to preserve

Rank badge with the paradise flycatcher, insignia of a civil official of the ninth rank, the design worked in fine Peking knot stitch on a ground entirely couched in gold-wrapped threads. c. 1850.

Man's chaofu, *rare ceremonial court robe. c. 1870.*

their culture and heritage, so they made their national costumes a symbol of authority and rule. The traditional Han Chinese court attire was banned and the Manchu imposed their national costumes on all who attended court. Thus the Manchu conquerors kept a separate ethnic identity through the regulation of costume. As the rulers of Heaven and Earth, however, the Qing emperors were obliged to continue the rites and ceremonies required by the mandate of Heaven. For this reason, the Manchus continued to use ancient Chinese imperial symbolism to decorate their robes.

WOMAN'S *CHAOFU*: FORMAL COURT DRAGON ROBE

The woman's formal *chaofu* is the only court costume to be cut with inset sleeves. Like the man's *chaofu*, it was based on traditional Manchu costume. The woman's *chaofu* is rarer than the man's *chaofu*, as there were fewer occasions on which it could be worn.

Woman's chaofu, *rare ceremonial court robe. There were five shades of yellow, and brown, being a 'lesser yellow', was worn by members of the imperial clan. This robe would have been made for a princess or noblewoman. c. 1770.*

BUFU : MANDARIN'S SURCOAT

Mandarins wore a plain, front-opening surcoat over their robes. This was made of dark blue silk, decorated only by a square badge on the front and back. The badge indicated the wearer's office and rank, either civil or military. This surcoat *(bufu)* covered the entire dragon robe, with only the *lishui* wave border visible at the bottom and the 'horseshoe' cuffs visible at the wrists. It seems strange that the sumptuously decorated dragon robes should have been entirely covered, but there was a reason for this. The Emperor Qianlong (reigned 1736-1795) wanted to remind his officials that the reason for wearing the dragon robe was not for outward pomp and circumstance, but rather for the inner spiritual power that the symbolism of the robe represented. It was Qianlong who passed the imperial edict specifying the code of dress to be worn at court. As with the *chaofu*, this simple coat was based on Manchu tradition.

Mandarin's surcoat, bufu, *with a rank badge insignia of a silver pheasant, which would have been worn by a fifth rank civil official.*

BUZI : RANK BADGES

The mandarin square, or rank badge, was an embroidered or woven square. It indicated which of the nine ranks of civil and military officials the wearer had attained. The official's wife always took on the rank of her husband and she would also wear a rank badge. Military officials wore badges showing an animal, while civil officials wore badges with a bird. The imperial family wore *bufu* with embroidered dragon roundels. The badge was either integrated onto the *bufu* during its manufacture or appliquéd, allowing the wearer to upgrade his rank without having to replace his coat. The practice of wearing these badges as official marks of rank first arose during the Yuan Dynasty (1279-1368), was continued by the Ming and then adopted by the Qing.

Kesi *rank badge showing a paradise flycatcher, the insignia of a ninth rank civil official. The design is worked in fine Peking knot stitch on a ground entirely couched in gold-wrapped threads. c. 1850.*

Civil officials had greater status than their military counterparts. It is believed that birds were chosen for the civil ranks because, having the ability to fly, they were regarded as being closer to Heaven and thus associated with literary talent and wisdom. By contrast, animals, although more physically powerful, were earthbound and considered less endowed in relation to knowledge. Each of the birds or animals is shown looking up towards a red sun, which authorities believe comes from the ancient proverb 'keep your eye on the sun and rise high'. The background is filled with clouds, bats, water, mountains and other auspicious symbols.

Civil Badges of Rank

First rank	Crane
Second rank	Golden pheasant
Third rank	Peacock
Fourth rank	Wild goose
Fifth rank	Silver pheasant
Sixth rank	Egret
Seventh rank	Mandarin duck
Eighth rank	Quail
Ninth rank	Paradise flycatcher

Dragon roundel from an imperial surcoat, 18th century.

Military Badges of Rank

Rank	Animal
First rank	Qilin*
Second rank	Lion
Third rank	Leopard
Fourth rank	Tiger
Fifth rank	Bear
Sixth rank	Panther
Seventh rank	Rhinoceros
Eighth rank	Rhinoceros
Ninth rank	Sea horse

* (*Qilin* is a mythical animal similar to a unicorn.)

Dark indigo silk rank badge showing a panther, the insignia of a sixth rank military official. It is worked in Peking knot and satin stitches, surrounded by stylized clouds, bats and Buddhist symbols, while the ground is gold couched with a scrolling fret pattern. c. 1860.

Kesi rank badge showing a bear, the insignia of a fifth rank military official. The bear is surrounded by bats, narcissi, peonies and the eight Buddhist symbols floating in the waves. c. 1860.

HATS AND SURKNOBS

The rules surrounding the official attire of the mandarin required the wearing of hats. The mandarin's winter hat was made of black felt, decorated with a red silk fringe and topped with a jewelled cap finial (surknob) at the crown. The summer hat was cone-shaped, made of stiffened cloth or woven cane, again festooned with red silk fringe and finial. The jewel set in the finial was also an indicator of rank.

Mandarin's winter hat with second rank coral surknob.

Mandarin's summer hat with seventh rank gold surknob.

Mandarin's winter boots.

Kesi rank badge showing a lion, the insignia of a second rank military official. The badge is worked entirely in fine Peking knot stitch on deep indigo satin. Surrounding the lion are clouds, bats, narcissi and auspicious symbols floating in the waves. c. 1800.

Kesi rank badge showing a tiger, the insignia of a fourth rank military official, worked in counted stitch on fine silk gauze. In the surrounding sky and waves are auspicious symbols, including Taoist and Buddhist emblems. c. 1870.

Deep indigo satin rank badge showing a leopard, the insignia of a third rank military official, worked in Peking knot stitch, with bats, peaches, peonies, narcissi, sacred fungus-shaped clouds and Taoist symbols. c. 1800.

Early Qing Dynasty rank badge showing a peacock, the insignia of a third rank civil official. Early Qing rank badges had fewer symbols and more open design than those of later rank badges. This rare example has a background of straight-laid gold couching, with couched peacock feather rock and satin stitch bird. c. 1680.

Kesi rank badge showing a mandarin duck, the insignia of a seventh rank civil official. In the surrounding sky are Taoist symbols, with Buddhist emblems floating in the waves. c. 1870.

Surknob Ranks

First rank	Transparent ruby
Second rank	Opaque coral
Third rank	Transparent sapphire
Fourth rank	Opaque lapis lazuli
Fifth rank	Transparent crystal
Sixth rank	Opaque jade
Seventh rank	Plain gold
Eighth rank	Worked gold with *shou* (longevity) character
Ninth rank	Worked gold with two *shou* characters

XIAPI : WOMAN'S CEREMONIAL COURT VEST

The *xiapi* was a long open waistcoat, attached at the sides with ribbons and decorated with dragons above a *lishui* wave border. These vests were usually embellished with a rank badge and sometimes their design incorporated the nine rank birds.

CHANGFU : INFORMAL DRAGON ROBE

The third style of dragon robe, the *changfu*, was worn for travelling and social gatherings when full formal attire was not required. For the Chinese red was the colour of joy and celebration. Red robes with auspicious symbols were worn at festivals like the lunar New Year, birthdays and weddings. A candidate who had just passed the imperial examinations would have worn a red robe with eight dragons. On her wedding day, a bride would wear a pleated silk skirt and a short red robe decorated with

This **kesi changfu,** *decorated with cranes (symbols of longevity), was probably made to be worn at a wedding or anniversary. Among the waves are woven pink peonies, emblems of riches and honour. c. 1870.*

This rare xiapi has no rank badge, but all
nine rank birds are shown in the surrounding sky. c. 1850.

dragons (masculine) and phoenix (feminine), reflecting the dual nature of the universe. The phoenix was said to have five colours of feathers, after the five cardinal virtues, and its song had five notes that resembled the music of pan pipes. This mythical bird represents *yin* (feminine energy), goodness and prosperity and became associated with the empress. The phoenix's appearance on the bridal gown indicated that the bride was 'empress for the day'.

WOMEN'S INFORMAL ROBES

Women, holding no office, were seldom required to participate in formal court assemblies or sacrificial ceremonies within the halls of the Forbidden City, except as invited spectators. When mandarins' wives were summoned to court for an official function, they wore robes reflecting the rank of their husbands.

While the men were required to wear Manchu-style garments for all official activities, women were not so constrained. Without such restrictions, women's robes, skirts, tunics, jackets, hats and shoes reflected the stylistic and ethnic diversity of the entire country. Many of the informal women's robes had the wide sleeves, cloud collar and front opening that was popular amongst the majority Han people of central China. Occasionally regional variations can be identified, such as the shades of lilac and pink loved by the Chaozhou people of Fujian Province in the southeast. Only the Han practised foot-binding and this had an influence on skirts and robes, which were cut to make them complementary to the 'lily feet'.

Some of the design elements of men's robes of state were incorporated in the women's robes worn for important occasions, such as the *lishui* wave border and a broader version of the Manchu horseshoe cuff.

For more informal occasions, three-quarter length robes and short jackets were worn with pleated wrap-around skirts. Auspicious symbols were either woven into the silk or embroidered onto the costume, with designs such as mandarins with their ladies in pavilioned gardens, surrounded by lakes, rivers, flowering trees, rocks and distant mountains. All embroidered decoration had symbolic meaning and any educated person of that period would have read the juxtaposition of symbols on a robe like poetry. They would have known that the peony was the flower of riches and honour, and the butterfly an emblem of happiness carrying the message 'May your troubles be as light as a butterfly's wing'.

Red silk shoes for bound feet, embroidered with flowers. Han Chinese women had their feet bound from an early age to keep them small. Such 'lily feet' were considered beautiful. c. 1880.

Han Chinese-style woman's short robe and pleated skirt. The robe, complete with sleevebands, shows embroidered imperial dragon boats festooned with ceremonial canopies and banners. The light blue damask skirt is also embroidered with peonies and lotus flowers (purity). The traditional Han Chinese skirt consisted of a pair of pleated aprons, with embroidered panels back and front. It was wrapped around the waist and fixed with a cord. The side pleating added weight and flexibility, which allowed the skirt to flow attractively when the wearer walked on bound feet. This created the 'willow-swaying walk' considered by Han Chinese men as the epitome of feminine beauty. Both c. 1870.

Woman's informal robe of indigo silk damask. Trimmed with a black and gold wan-fret border, the sleevebands elaborately embroidered in Peking knot stitch on a gold couched background. c. 1860

Woman's informal robe of dark indigo silk, embroidered with a design of scrolling lotus and butterflies. c. 1850.

Woman's informal robe of embroidered blue satin silk. The roundels show women in garden pavilions, engaged in scholarly pursuits, playing music or chess, painting and conversing— suitable occupations for an idyllic life of refinement. Scattered around the robe are auspicious plants, including the peony, lotus, gourd, narcissus, plum blossom and chrysanthemum. c. 1860.

Sleevebands

Sleevebands, the most important of the trimmings on the robe, were often characterized by extremely delicate, detailed embroidery. One or two sets of sleevebands could be sewn on the outside of the sleeve. These smaller items often came from an embroidery studio that specialized in accessories. A tailor, visiting a client about to choose a new set of robes, would have brought along a sample book of trimmings, sleevebands and collars. Sometimes an additional set of sleevebands was sewn into the inside of the sleeves, so they could be seen when the sleeves were folded back. Every conceivable colour, design and material was used, often contrasting with the design of the garment itself.

A collection of exquisitely embroidered 19th-century sleevebands.

TECHNIQUES: THE MAKING OF A ROBE

Robes and trimmings were woven and embroidered as yardage and then made up for the wearer as he or she needed them. Many of the court robes were made in the imperial workshops. Others would have been made by a mandarin's wives, concubines and daughters.

Chinese looms wove strips of silk only three feet wide. Within this narrow yardage, the design was laid out so that the front of the robe formed a single piece with the back. The left and right sides were on two separate panels. The silk was laid out and the design carefully stencilled on, then the panels were stretched onto a frame about 12 feet long. A team of embroiderers would sit around the frame and sew the design. When all but the centre of the robe had been embroidered, the two sides were joined. The embroidery was then completed over the central seam. Afterwards the cuffs and trimmings were added and the garment finished.

The Chinese used various weaving and embroidery techniques to produce textiles that were, as Dong Qichang (1555-1636) wrote in Ming times, 'pictures better than painting'.

*Red **kesi** woman's robe, with large roundels of cranes, peonies, chrysanthemums and lotus flowers, while at the hem of the robe is the **lishui** border. The wide horseshoe cuffs, a typical style of the late Qing Dynasty, are woven with a black ground, as are the trimmings. c. 1870.*

A woman's informal summer robe of red silk gauze embroidered with peonies and butterflies in counted stitch. Peonies represent riches and honour while the butterfly symbolizes beauty, happiness and longevity—"May your troubles be as light as a butterfly's wing". c. 1890

A woman's two-tiered 'cloud collar', Han Chinese, embroidered onto a stiffened silk backing with a design of auspicious flowers and butterflies. Very often these collars were in the same shop as sleevebands and other trimmings and applied to a finished robe. c. 1870.

Peking knot stitch, also called *dazi* (meaning 'making seeds'), is a circular knotted stitch which resembles a seed and was used to fill design shapes. It was also called the 'forbidden stitch', because it was used on imperial court costumes in the Forbidden City.

Couching was an embroidery technique in which threads were laid on top of the material and tacked down with fine stitching. The usual thread used for couching was gold-wrapped silk floss. This is untwisted silk floss (raw silk yarn), which has 24-carat gold leaf twisted around it in a helix fashion. One hundred per cent of the outer area of the thread would, therefore, be covered with pure gold. Peacock feather was sometimes used instead of gold for rare and special pieces. Gold couching was also used to delineate the dragon, because this technique could produce a three-dimensional effect of serpentine scales.

Brocade's polychrome designs were achieved by alternating warps of two different colours, which together created a compound double-weave, richly luxurious fabric. However, for these compound weaves to be produced, it was necessary to use a loom similar to the modern Jacquard loom. The Chinese invented, probably in the late Zhou Dynasty (c. 600 BC), a two-person operated 'drawloom', which comprised a tremendously complex group of drawbundles in a definite order, as prescribed by the design. If only two alternating colours were used, the fabric would be reversible. There are existing examples of polychrome brocades, woven at a density of 156 threads per centimetre or almost 400 threads to the inch, as early as the Warring States Period (475-221BC).

Pigments and **dyes** were used to make many hues and shades and an elaborate, multi-stage dyeing process was developed. By the time of the Zhou Dynasty, bleaching, dyeing and printing was a highly specialized industry. By the Qin Dynasty (221-206 BC) as many as seven steps in a dyeing process had been documented. The dyes and pigments were as follows:

Red	– madder
Blue	– indigo
Yellow	– gardenia flowers
White	– sericite
Silver-grey	– lead sulphide
Vermilion	– cinnabar

Kesi (literally 'engraved thread') was the most elaborate type of tapestry weave practised in China, the design made up in one piece on a large loom. The technique was probably incorporated from the Uighur and Turkic peoples of Central Asia, around the beginning of the Song Dynasty in about AD960. It is often called the 'Chinese Silk Gobelin', though *kesi* is many times finer. The finest French Gobelins have been counted at 22 weft threads per centimetre, while the Chinese *kesi* has 114. The Chinese developed incredible skill at this most demanding, elaborate and subtle of textile techniques.

SYMBOLISM IN CHINESE GARMENTS

Each symbol on the court robes had a meaning and the garments could be read like poetry. Often the auspicious symbols were a play on words. For example, the words for bat and happiness are both pronounced *fu*, but written in a different way.

Detail showing the Peking knot stitch.

A finely woven kesi robe, with double happiness symbols worked in silver, against a blue ground woven with a gold wan (Chinese character for ten thousand) fret design. c.1850.

Uncut chifu, *the entire background worked with couched peacock feather.*

The eight Buddhist emblems of good fortune

Canopy
the monarch

Conch shell
the call to worship

Sacred vase
holds the water of life
and also means peace

Umbrella
the incorruptible
official

Lotus flower
purity

Wheel of law
the ever-turning cycle
of the transmigration
of souls

Endless knot
long life and the
everlasting love of
Buddha

Pair of fish
abundance

The attributes of the Eight Immortals

When these symbols are grouped together, they mean the successful search
for immortality and wishes for good fortune:

The fan carried by
Zhongli Quan

The sword of
Lu Dongbin

The double gourd and
crutch of Li Tieguai

The castanets of
Cao Guojiu

The basket of peaches
of Lan Caihe

The bamboo tube and
rods of Zhang Guolao

The flute of Han
Xiangzi

The lotus pod of He
Xiangu

Characters as symbols of good fortune

Shou
longevity

Wan
ten thousand

Xi
joy

Ji
luck

Shuangxi
double happiness

 Swastika
Buddha's heart, longevity and ten thousand

Imperial rank badge with gourd and canopy, worn for the Lantern Festival and New Year. Late Ming Dynasty, 17th century.

Symbols of wealth and fortune

Any eight of these treasures, when grouped together, are called 'eight precious things' or *ba bao*.

 Lingzhi fungus
longevity

 Pair of rectangular gold ornaments

 Cloud
peace and good fortune

 Pair of circular gold ornaments

 Ruyi sceptre
'as you wish'

 Pearl

 Ruyi sceptre with swastika
'may you have everything you wish'

 Pair of scrolls

 Musical stone

 Pair of rhinoceros horns

 Ruyi sceptre with scroll motif
'good wishes for a long life and all you desire'

 Coral

 Ingot

Fauna and Flora

 Crane
longevity, majesty and wisdom

 Mandarin ducks
faithfulness and marital happiness

 Peacock
splendour

 **Bat**
happiness

Brocade detail.

Bat with peaches
'may you live long and be happy'

Bat with swastika
'may you have the greatest joy'

Pine tree
longevity, majesty and wisdom

Peaches
longevity

'Buddha's hand' citron
happiness and longevity

Pomegranate
fertility in one's offspring, sons and a long lineage

The Three Plenties
a combination of peaches, 'Buddha's hand' citron and pomegranate

Butterfly
longevity, summer, marital happiness and beauty

Prunus
first month, winter, perseverance and purity

Peony
sixth month, spring, wealth and advancement

Lotus
seventh month, summer, purity and nobility

Chrysanthemum
tenth month, autumn, reclusiveness, gentility, fellowship, nobility and longevity

Orchid
eleventh month, charm in seclusion, friendship and nobility

Narcissus
twelfth month, good fortune, purity, cleanliness and prosperity.